CREATING SMALL CHRISTIAN COMMUNITIES

Minimum Structure, Maximum Life

**by Barbara A. Darling
with Jack Ventura, SM**

Good Ground Press
Publishers of *Sunday by Sunday*
1884 Randolph Avenue
St. Paul, Minnesota 55105

Contents

The Essentials of Church
Social Time

Configuration of Groups
Affinity Groups
Family Small Christian Communities

Introducing Small Groups Parish Wide

Keeping the Vision Alive

Summing Up Practical Suggestions

Prayer

CHAPTER 3
_____

Initiating Non-Parish Communities of Faith
by Jack Ventura, SM

The First Small Faith Community

Four Examples of Small Communities of Faith
Religious Evangelical Community
Christian Family Community of Faith
Ministry or Profession Faith Communities
Marginalized Communities

The Process of Forming a Non-Parish-Based
Small Faith Community
Identifying Founders, Animators
A Beginning Step-by-Step Approach
Ongoing Community

Prayer

APPENDIX
_____

Introduction

Since the early 20th century, contemporary small Christian communities or small communities of faith have evolved in all parts of the globe. Ian Fraser, author, researcher, and member of the Iona Community in Scotland since 1938, suggests this development of small Christian communities "is the result of the spontaneous combustion of the Holy Spirit all over the world."

No one can capture or control the "combustion of the Holy Spirit," so neither can this book offer a readymade program to implement or precise plan to follow. José Marins, a Brazilian priest and internationally-known, small-community advisor and speaker, inspires our purpose in his observation that small Christian communities need a minimum of structure and a maximum of life. Our book aims to present potential structures and invite readers to choose the possibilities that will maximize the life of any communities they accompany and animate.

As authors, we bring to this project our experience of many small communities—those with whom Barb has worked in her years as executive director of the U. S. Buena Vista Network, the communities who participated in the international consultations through Notre Dame's Kellogg Center under Bob Pelton's leadership, and the many Marianist communities that Jack's religious order, the Society of Mary, has generated. No perfect formula or program exists. People, parishes, small groups, localities, situations all vary. Every person brings to the work of forming a community diverse experiences, insights, gifts, and perceptions. We have gathered wisdom from the small Christian communities we know. Those who want to form small Christian communities will need to tailor the processes we outline to fit their own situations.

Small Christian communities (SCCs) form in at least three different ways.

First, parish-based communities. Many parishes initiate and in varying ways give ongoing support to small Christian communities. SCC members worship with the people of the sponsoring parish and contribute to its life. These communities may begin as temporary or seasonal study or faith-sharing groups and use resource materials that the parish designs or chooses. They understand themselves linked to the universal Church as units of the parish. People in some parish-based communities may commit to a long-term relationship, begin to take responsibility for their own life as a community, and develop Church connections beyond the parish, but at the same time stay very connected to parish life.

Second, non-parish-based communities. Most commonly, these communities of faith cross parish boundaries and don't depend on support from one particular parish. Usually participants return to a chosen parish for Sunday Eucharist and may actively connect with that parish. These groups do not gather for the purpose of building up their parish life; rather they form around inter-parish experiences such as a Cursillo or the Christian Family Movement or through association with a religious community and its religious charism or spirituality.

Third, communities on the margin. Also a non-parish-based model are communities that gather outside traditional parish structures. Some refer to these groups as "communities on the margins" of traditional church life. They may be ecumenical or cross-congregational. Usually these communities have no desire to connect with a parish as a group.

All these communities share commonalities of faith and structure. We who create and participate in small communities must believe in and listen to one another. We must create opportunities to bond and build community. We must be agents of action rather than objects of action. At the core of each community must be one unalterable truth: that we are of God, doing God's work and bringing forth God's kingdom. The concept of small church is still being born, still in the creation stage with the boundless energy and spontaneity of the Spirit very much in charge.

Whatever kind of community you seek to form, you will benefit from reading all three chapters of this book. In our experience communities share more common characteristics than differences in their vision and practice.

Barb Darling
Jack Ventura, SM

Applause to Joan Mitchell, CSJ, Therese Sherlock, CSJ, and the other folks at Good Ground Press for supporting small Christian communities through their publications. Special thanks to the following people for encouragement and for sharing their wisdom: Barbara Howard and the core team and SCC members at Spirit of Christ Catholic Community; Carol Blank, José Marins, Paul O'Bryan, Nora Petersen, Irene Wilson, Felicia Wolf, OSF, Joe Healey, MM, and too many folks to list in SCCs around the world. And, of course, the Oilers (Barb's small Christian community of 30 years in Arvada, Colorado).

Glossary of Terms

A bewildering abundance of names and terms surround SCCs, expressing often subtle differences in charism or purpose. At this point many terms have no single definitions. This glossary describes the ways we use and understand these terms in this book.

When people refer to a *faith-sharing group*, they are often talking about short-term groups—Advent or Lenten gatherings or groups totally dependent on the parish for their existence and direction.

The terms *small church community, neighborhood church, house church, small communities of faith, intentional community, basic ecclesial community* usually refer to groups of people who have a history together and have made a long-term commitment to be church for each other and for the larger world. Parish efforts may have initiated these communities and they may connect with the large Church, but they have taken on a life of their own and will continue to meet even if parish support is withdrawn.

The term *neighborhood church* is beginning to take on new meaning, especially in Australia, where Mass attendance is declining drastically. In this model of basic community, parishes are attempting to re-establish contact with 100% of the Catholics in an area of 100–150 households through door-to-door visiting, small-group activities, and sacramental programs. This model aims to build or rebuild relationships.

In many countries in Africa and Latin America and in the Philippines, where parishes are massive and people often live in remote villages, the multi-layer parish has emerged with each of several *neighborhood church* communities offering Sunday liturgy and establishing in turn additional small communities for faith sharing. We regard the terms *small Christian community, small community, small church, small community of faith* and *small group* as interchangeable and generic. Jack relies on the term *small community of faith* in chapter three as he describes non-parish-based communities, which are often ecumenical and even cross the boundaries of the Christian faith.

The terms *animator* and *accompanier* describe those who encourage others to "catch" the spirit of small Christian community—a resource person, a promoter, a minister of welcome and support. These persons explore, hold, and pass on the vision of SCCs; they accompany and support the encompassing plan of community. We used these words, which are more common in other parts of our global Church than the United States, because they go beyond the roles of leader or organizer or coordinator to connote a gentler peer relationship. In chapter three Jack uses the term *founder* to mean the person who generates interest in forming a community. All founders need to be animators but not all animators are founders.

More specifically, this book refers to *accompaniers* as the group of staff and/or volunteers (the core group or core team) who accompany a number of SCCs. *Animators* are persons who embrace and pass on the vision within each group. Many refer to these folks as pastoral facilitators or facilitators. In this book we use the term *facilitator* to denote the one(s) who guides a particular session of a small Christian community or small community of faith.

CHAPTER ONE

Understanding Small Christian Communities

They devoted themselves to the apostles' instruction and the communal life, to the breaking of bread and the prayers. Those who believed shared all things in common. They went to the temple area together every day, while in their homes they broke bread. With exultant and sincere hearts they took their meals in common, praising God and winning the approval of all the people. Day by day the Lord added to their number those who were being saved.   Acts 3.42, 44, 46-47

These verses from the Acts of the Apostles describe Christian communities of faith in both the early centuries and in our time. Early Christians gathered in household or neighborhood groups to live the teaching and new vision that the risen Jesus brought them. They sought and found the kingdom of God he announced in their midst. In Dura-Europa, a town on the Euphrates River, archaeologists found a house church dating from AD 250, in which about 120 people could gather.

When the Emperor Constantine legalized Christianity in the Roman Empire, AD 313, he gave empty public buildings (basilicas) to these burgeoning small churches to meet in or he built new basilicas. These buildings were too large for the more intimate sharing possible in homes. Eventually Christian communities used these buildings only to celebrate the Eucharist and other sacraments; the church became a place to "come and receive." Parishes as we know them today arose in the Middle Ages out of the authority structure and patronage customs of the feudal system. In contemporary times, we live in the shadows of giant Gothic cathedrals and the sprawl of mega-churches still yearning for what the earliest Christians experienced—face-to-face sharing of our faith and our lives and prayer together, praising God "with exultant and sincere hearts."

To recapture the early Christian experience, it is tempting to choose a resource especially created for spiritual small groups, invite some folks, and found a small Christian community. This direct approach works for some, and there is something to be said for the just-do-it attitude. In my experience more preparation is desirable to build enduring small church. To develop healthy small groups and nurture long-term, small Christian communities, those who want to create a community can benefit from understanding where they are heading and what they are asking of participants. How can a larger picture of what is going on in community help us? What can we learn from the experience of those who have gone this way before us?

Building understanding becomes the first stage in creating a small Christian community. This involves both discerning one's personal and local situation and exploring the history and vision of SCCs.

Discerning Your Personal Situation

Motives for Community

Anyone ready to form a small Christian community must identify what motivates this desire and interest. Animators and prospective participants need to have realistic expectations of a group. Some examples of suitable motives include:

> ➤ to facilitate participants' quest to discover and nurture their own spirituality;

> ➤ to help people connect their faith to their daily lives;

> ➤ to connect people with one another and God's word;

➤ to enable participants to understand their place in the worldwide church;

➤ to nurture learning communities of faith that enable the
church to witness to family, neighborhood, and society;

➤ to fulfill an unmet spiritual need;

➤ to make a difference in ourselves and in the world around us.

Some examples of unsuitable motives are:

➤ to develop a readily available and committed work force for
the parish;

➤ to provide another program for the parish and add to the
number of parishioners involved in ministry;

➤ to provide a preaching forum for passionate Christians.

Joseph Healey, a Maryknoll Missioner who has devoted his life to
accompanying small Christian communities in East Africa, has dis-
covered "a new disturbing trend in weekly SCC meetings (notice-
able especially in Dar es Salaam and Nairobi), away from sharing
reflections/comments on the bible text and towards a
preaching/teaching style." After his research in East Africa in 2002
and 2003, he notes, "This is definitely an influence of the charismat-
ic/pentecostal style of bible teaching, but is NOT appropriate for the
bible reflection process of the SCC meetings." [1]

When one person becomes the teacher in a group, the community
becomes a class rather than a community in which all have voice
and the Spirit moves in each for the common good. Bernard Lee's
Lilly-supported study of small Christian communities reports that
although three fourths of the small Christian communities are parish
connected, leadership rests in the community and members participate in making decisions.[2]

Expectations of Community

The longing for a spiritual community is such a worthwhile desire
it is hard to imagine all the unrealistic and unarticulated expectations

we can harbor. The experience of other small communities can help express unconscious expectations and identify common pitfalls.

To discover and connect with others who already have a small community, call neighborhood churches, diocesan offices, and be open to whispers of the Spirit. Join one of the national organizations that network SCCs (See the *Appendix*). Even if no SCC activity appears to thrive in your vicinity, you will be surprised what you learn if you keep your ear to the ground at your workplace, at coffee houses, or standing in line at the grocery. Small Christian communities are grassroots circles of folks that are not always on parish or diocesan mailing lists. The opportunity to pool resources and knowledge, share ideas and encouragement with a wider network is mutually beneficial and worth finding. Prayer is the most imperative part of the discernment process—seeking God's plan for you and being open to that fiery wisdom of the Spirit.

Some unrealistic or unconscious expectations of community are common enough to identify as pitfalls.

PITFALL 1: Organizing SCCs is a short-term or individual commitment. Letting one person take on all responsibility for organizing and sustaining SCCs in the parish may jeopardize the effort.

Too much reliance on the pastor or any other one person as the sole accompanier of small groups puts the groups at risk. Inevitably the pastor gets a new assignment or the responsible person moves on. This leaves small communities fending for themselves with no solid connection to each other or the larger Church. The goal of community is to nurture the larger vision in each participant, including shared responsibility for the group.

PITFALL 2: Our pastor must be a vital proponent of SCCs.

Many pastors understand the concept of small community and do everything possible to encourage their evolution without taking any responsibility for their development. Some lucky organizers work with a pastor willing to be available as an integral and equal participant of the planning team and of a small community itself. Some

SCC organizers feel lucky if their pastor simply agrees not to block their efforts. Other pastors attach a program mentality to small communities and assign a staff person to add this ministry to a growing list of responsibilities, reporting back to him from time to time.

PITFALL 3: A small Christian community is a good way to interact with others who believe and think as I do.

Many people find sustaining support for their faith and prayer lives in small communities, but in no group of people does everyone think, feel, or act the same. Every individual affects the dynamic of a small community. In his book *Why We Live In Community*, Eberhard Arnold says, "Groups of people who would never have chosen to be together in an ordinary human way find themselves together. It is a test of faith. It puts God's love to the test and it is meant to. It is what Saint Paul means. It isn't just a question of whether you are building community with people that you naturally like; it is also a question of building community with people that God has brought together."[3]

PITFALL 4: Every SCC gathering will be stimulating.

SCCs can be reduced to one more meeting to attend if we forget our vision. Community is not about meetings but about communion and mission.

PITFALL 5: We will overcome disagreements and difficult times easily because we are a group committed to building God's kingdom.

The reality is that despite all our best efforts, setbacks will happen. Most assuredly conflict will occur. No matter how diligently founders plan, some communities won't make it. I sometimes wonder how many communities Paul founded that fell apart and never made it into the New Testament.

Exploring the SCC Vision

When local discernment encourages our hope to start a small Christian community, it is time to learn more about the larger, global vision of small Christian communities. SCC people affirm there is no absolutely right definition of small Christian community. José Marins, a theologian who travels the world encouraging the efforts of small church, addressed our natural desire for a blueprint when he keynoted Buena Vista's 10th Convocation in 1996.

Jesus didn't leave a recipe for small Christian communities with his disciples. We want a blueprint at the least. People want to know "What do I do?" But it is more of a challenge than that to build SCCs. The early communities of Christians had one goal, the reign of God, and then they learned how to act in different ways in different cultures.

We also need the same goal—the reign of God. Then we must consider our culture, our situation, the individuals we are dealing with, and the methods we will use. Only the goal is always the same. The people, methods, and pastoral options change as we discern and choose our actions and priorities.

Although we cannot define or confine small Christian communities, some communities have described beneficial criteria and healthy patterns to point us in the right direction.

Beneficial Criteria

In Eastern Africa the bishops have adopted criteria to use in evaluating a typical SCC. Many of these guidelines are universal and appropriate for a small group in any country to consider. With permission I have adapted their guidelines for our purpose.

➤ The SCC is small. Usually not more than 15 or so adults attend regularly (perhaps with a varying number of children) and meet in the home of one of its members on a rotating basis.

➤ The SCC is the felt need of its members on the local level without depending on a priest or pastoral worker.

➤ The SCC tries to form and evolve from the grassroots—out of the daily life and experience of the people themselves.

➤ The SCC chooses its leaders/ministers from within.

➤ The SCC emphasizes personal relationships, solidarity, and Christian belonging.

➤ The SCC chooses a name that gives the group a specific Christian identity beyond its geographical place or facilitator's name.

➤ The SCC has some kind of scripture sharing and reflection on a regular basis. Often communities choose the gospel of the following Sunday. With a clear step-by-step plan members try to integrate faith and life, prayer, the scripture, and everyday experience.

➤ The SCC members participate in liturgy with the larger community.

➤ The SCC has some kind of planned practical action, mutual aid, and social outreach which responds to local challenges and problems.

➤ The SCC analyzes justice and peace issues with concrete follow-up on the SCC, parish, and wider levels.

➤ The SCC participates in the parish structures with various pastoral responsibilities, decisions, and activities in the parish especially related to its members' religious education and preparation for receiving the sacraments.

➤ There are regular meetings and training sessions of the SCC leaders.

➤ There is some kind of coordination and networking of the different SCCs on the parish, diocesan, and wider levels.[4]

The Eastern African Church gives priority to SCCs and makes them an integral part of all parish and diocesan pastoral plans. Regrettably in the United States there is little widespread parish pastoral planning for SCCs, with a few notable exceptions, and few diocesan-wide pastoral plans that include them.

Healthy Patterns

Healthy small Christian communities include these traits:

➤ Connections to the larger church and community;

➤ Welcoming and inviting attitudes;

➤ Catechesis and formation;

➤ Shared principles and objectives;

➤ Scripture, prayer, and transformational action.

CONNECTIONS Small Christian community is connection. In community we are about being in communion with the other members of our small group. That connection in turn implies that our group connects with others in the larger Church and community.

In his 1998 post-synodal exhortation, *Ecclesia in America*, Pope John Paul II focuses specifically on connections between small Christian communities and the larger Church. First, he recognizes, "Today in America as elsewhere in the world the parish is facing certain difficulties in fulfilling its mission" (137). He recommends small Christian communities as a way to reestablish human relationships in church communities:

> *It seems timely therefore to form ecclesial communities and groups of a size that allows for true human relationships [in] the parish to which such groups belong, and with the entire diocesan and universal Church. In such a human context, it will be easier to gather to hear the Word of God, to reflect on the range of human problems in the light of this Word, and gradually to make responsible decisions inspired by the all-embracing love of Christ* (141).

In his global vision of the effect of small Christian communities on parishes, the Holy Father writes, "The institution of the parish, thus renewed, can be the source of great hope. It can gather people in community, assist family life, overcome the sense of anonymity, welcome people and help them to be involved in their neighborhood and in society" (142).

Patrick Kalilombe, M.Afr, a bishop of Malawi, sees the mission of the small Christian community to be active builders of church, not passive consumers of church. In the 2002 international consultation at the University of Notre Dame, entitled *The Spirituality of Small Christian Communities Around the Globe*, Bishop Kalilombe insisted, "In order to have an effective church we ought not be just receivers of ministry and sacrament but instead we must develop parishes and communities which are self-ministering, self-propagating, and self-supporting."[5]

In other words, the community and therefore the parish and diocese arise from the passion of the people and not only from the top down. If our baptism makes us church and gives us this gift also as our work and mission, then we cannot wait for "the Church" to take responsibility for organizing us into communities, into this very basic unit of church that we the people of God can form. In turn, the people of God also have the responsibility to support and develop healthy parishes and dioceses.

SCC Twinning is one way in which communities can look outside themselves to the larger experience of community and church. The twinning process introduces SCCs to a community in another culture and country and encourages participants to build a reciprocal relationship of prayer and spiritual encouragement, sharing faith and culture for mutual benefit.

Learning about church and community in other cultures enlarges our vision of small Christian community. We have much to learn from each other in the global Church. Several resources listed in the *Appendix* are particularly helpful—the *Global Research SCC Project* published at www.buenavista.org; the video *It's a Small Church After All* from Buena Vista; and *An Experience of World Church in Miniature*, available from the Diocese of Hartford, 860-243-9642.

WELCOMING AND INVITING Community and communion are inclusive, open, other-centered terms; not exclusive or inward-looking. Some communities practice the simple tradition of incorporating an empty chair in all group gatherings to remind each other of the isolated and lonely people in the world. Because SCCs normally meet in homes, it is not practical to invite everyone who wishes to join (and besides, we're talking about *small* community!). What matters most within communities is a welcoming and inviting attitude toward differing points of view and toward other communities and individuals.

In the diocese of Adelaide, Australia, Basic Ecclesial Communities (BECs) are a vital component of the diocesan plan. Archbishop Leonard Faulkner proposes a vision of communities as church at the neighborhood level where people can gather in face-to-face community. He clearly connects outreach with communion. "It is fundamental to the BECs," he writes, "that they reach out to and involve people who are not regularly involved with the Sunday celebrations of the Eucharist, but this outreach springs from and is directed towards Eucharistic communion."[6]

The BECs in Adelaide experience the doorstep encounter in which small community members reach out to their neighbors as important to their own faith.

The encounters on the doorstep have been significant moments of conversion both for those visiting and those being visited. Those visiting must overcome a culturally-conditioned fear of outreach and involvement with those who are not necessarily "like" them in age, culture, interests, personality, or lifestyle. They go as representatives of their local parish, witnessing to a church that seeks to reconcile itself with those who are no longer actively involved in a worshiping community, as well as to strengthen the relationships between those who are currently involved. Many agree to take on this role because their hearts are touched by those who are isolated or abandoned in our local neighbourhoods and they dream of a church which can be experienced as a place of meaning and acceptance. The visiting imbues them with a stronger sense of their own mission to "be church" for others in the ordinary encounters of everyday life. The reaction of those being visited ranges from warmth and delight to mild curiosity and only occasionally irritation and hostility. Many respond with great hospitality and evident concern for those doing the visiting! An oft-heard refrain is "It's about time the Catholic Church did something like this." For a lot of people, it is their first experience of someone from the church listening to and caring about them for many years. The visiting is an essential part of the praxis of the BEC—it is both formation and action towards community building.[7]

CATECHESIS AND FORMATION We have an obligation to continue forming ourselves in God's image if small Christian communities are about building God's kingdom. The bishops of the United States put new emphasis on adult faith formation in their 1999 document *Our Hearts Were Burning Within Us*. They see small Christian communities as a natural setting in which adults can nourish one another.

Small communities are powerful vehicles for adult faith formation, providing opportunities for learning, prayer, mutual support, and the shared experience of Christian living and service to Church and society (#106).

The Office of Small Christian Communities, Diocese of Oakland, regularly prints booklets for the small communities in their diocese to use. Each book offers faith sharing on scripture as well as a section dedicated to church teaching. Nora Petersen, Director of the Department of Parish Resources and Specialist in Small Christian Communities, believes, "adults have the desire to learn more about their church and connect to the wisdom of the larger community. So we regularly include little stories about saints and quotes from them as well as relevant paragraphs from the *Catechism* or Vatican II documents in our booklets."

SHARED PRINCIPLES AND OBJECTIVES In my book, *Getting A Grip On Your Group; A Guide for Discerning Priorities in Your Small Christian Community*, I emphasize that members of a community need to agree about why they gather and what they do when they gather. "However a group originally forms, it is imperative that the members pause at regular intervals to recognize and assess their intention to gather and review their actions and activities."[8] This is something groups each need to do for themselves. The *Appendix* of this book includes a simple initial agreement that members of a small group can use. However, when a group has gathered for a while and wants to consider making a longer-term commitment, the members will want to draw up their own guiding principles, using the process outlined in *Getting a Grip* or a similar process.

THE UNIVERSALITY OF SCRIPTURE Scripture is universal to Christians everywhere, our common inheritance. For this reason, scripture easily serves in new groups as a mutual basis for reflection and at the same time helps communities find their place in the global Church. A recent study of small Christian communities representing 14 countries on six continents found scripture is the linking energy among SCCs worldwide. Father Robert Pelton reflects on this phenomenon in the *Kellogg Institute Newsletter*. The Kellogg Institute at Notre Dame has undertaken the four international consultations on SCCs under Father Pelton's leadership. He writes:

> *Perhaps the leavening of these grassroots Christian communities across the globe is best illustrated by the fact that with no prompting, one in four of the SCCs in the total sample who reported a favorite and/or self-descriptive scriptural text chose the second and fourth chapter of Acts. It is paraphrased by the Beatitudes Community in Mexico: 'The crowd of the faithful had one single heart and soul. No one considered as theirs what they had; they had everything in common. God confirmed with his might the testimony of the apostles as to Jesus Christ's resurrection and they all lived something wonderful.*[9]

Good lectionary-based materials provide a meeting structure indispensable for beginning small groups. All groups eventually flesh out their time together to meet their particular needs. But starting with a well-written resource such as those listed in the *Appendix* help communities stay on track and habitually include the essentials of prayer, scripture, ongoing learning, and transformational action along with suggestions for vigorous connections to larger Church and community.

PRAYER AND RITUAL Members come to community with varying degrees of experience with spontaneously spoken prayer. There are many ways to pray, and none of them is wrong. Prayer is laughing together, prayer is silent, prayer is singing, prayer is eloquent, prayer is faltering. Prayer and ritual can include dancing and crying and rosary beads. Prayer expresses gratitude, begs forgiveness, praises, and requests. It is often messy but God listens to our prayers however they are expressed. Whether we read from a prayer book or share our own words aloud, the important thing about prayer in community is that we do it together and accept all the different ways our members wish to express their prayer.

TRANSFORMATIONAL ACTION Much of what community is about is the inner life of the group—the ongoing learning, praying, faith sharing, reflecting on scripture and life, developing of the group's guiding principles. These are normally accomplished within the group, behind closed doors, shall we say. To be complete as a healthy small Christian community, we also need to grapple with the meaning of our public face.

Most communities find it easy to reach out to those in need through parish and local community efforts. Working at shelters, food banks, adopting families for holidays, are good and necessary works that don't go unnoticed.

The larger dilemma is working for justice. Uncovering the reasons for the needs we find in the larger world community and working to address those needs is the more difficult task. Perhaps changing ourselves is the most difficult task.

After attending a 1999 international gathering of small Christian community people from six continents, Brother Bob Moriarty, SM (Diocese of Hartford) was prompted to write:

While the consultation was a remarkable experience at any number of levels, its setting in Bolivia calls for special notice. This North American first-time visitor to South America can not help but acknowledge at the outset the impact of directly encountering the grinding poverty that so defines the concrete context of the developing world. It presents itself as a powerful reminder that we never do church in a vacuum. . . We have a church because we have a mission. And that mission is concerned not only with the transformation of individual hearts in coming to know Jesus as Lord, but also with the promotion of structures of justice and peace so that God may be "all in all" in a transformed world.[10]

In the Bronx, New York, a group of Spanish-speaking women aged 35-65 have been meeting as a small Christian community since 1993. The majority of the group is Catholic; most of them are bilingual; several of them are illiterate. The women are all active in the various parishes/churches to which they belong. They exemplify what a small Christian community can do together to promote systemic change.

The opportunity to share their faith and life is fundamental after all these years and they are very proud to have learned to put their faith into action as well. In one instance they were able to shut down incinerators of industrial and medical waste, which were causing a high incidence of asthma in the South Bronx. The ladies coordinated bus trips from the neighborhood to various hospitals in the city where television news teams recorded peaceful demonstrations meant to educate the hospital administrators and the public about the dangerous health situation in their neighborhood. Once the incinerators were closed they hosted workshops to help asthma victims understand their illness and the treatment available.[11]

Healthy small Christian communities connect in communion and mission with the whole Church. Their welcoming and inviting attitudes toward each other extend into the larger community as they engage the work of charity and justice locally and globally. Small Christian communities mix thought and practice, new ideas and members' long-standing faith commitments. They become ever widening circles of conversion to Jesus' continuing mission in the world and the Spirit's fiery urging toward action and communion.

PRAYER

Gracious God, we are grateful
for the spontaneity of Spirit among us.
Hold us within the breath of your wisdom
as we discern the particular path of our community.
Remind us to be of God in all things
and to be church among others
in the ordinary encounters of daily life. Amen

Endnotes

[1] Joseph Healey, MM, "Twelve Case Studies of Small Christian Communities (SCCs) in Eastern Africa," *How Local Is the Local Church; Small Christian Communities and Church in Eastern Africa*, Agatha R. Adoli, ed. (Eldoret: Spearhead No. 126-28: 59-103).

[2] Bernard J. Lee, SM, *The Catholic Experience of Small Christian Communities* (Mahwah, New Jersey: Paulist Press, 2000).

[3] Eberhard Arnold, *Why We Live in Community* (UK: Plough Publishing). No longer in print.

[4] Healey, *Op. Cit.*

[5] Rt. Rev. P.A. Kalilombe, M. Afr. From a report entitled "Building Small Christian Communities in a Changing Culture: The Case of Malawi," consultation entitled The Spirituality of Small Christian Communities Around the Globe, November, 2002, University of Notre Dame.

[6] Paul O'Bryan, Susan Holoubek, Emilio Biosca, OFM CAP, "Oceania Report," International SCC Consultation, Cochabamba, Bolivia, 1999.

[7] *Ibid.*

[8] Barbara A. Darling, *Getting a Grip on Your Group: A Guide for Discerning Priortieis in Your Small Christian Community* (St. Paul, Minnesota: Good Ground Press, 2002).

[9] Robert F. Pelton, CSC, "A Small Community, A World of Spirituality," *Kellogg Institute Newsletter*, Winter: 2003, No. 39 (South Bend, Indiana: University of Notre Dame) 16.

[10] Robert K. Moriarty, S.M., *An Experience of World Church in Miniature*, Diocese of Hartford.

[11] Robert Pelton, Nancy Reissner, Barbara Darling, eds., "Global Small Christian Community Research Project: Latin American/North American Church Concerns" University of Notre Dame and the Center for Mission Research and Study at Maryknoll, 2002. Access this research at: www.buenavista.org.

CHAPTER TWO

Initiating Small Christian Communities in Your Parish

*Greetings from Paul, a prisoner of Jesus Christ. . . to the
church that meets in your house. Grace to you and peace from
God our Father and from the Lord Jesus Christ. I always
thank my God as I remember you in my prayers because I hear
about your faith in the Lord Jesus and your love for all the
saints. I pray that you may be active in sharing your faith, so
that you will have a full understanding of every good thing we
have in Christ.*

Philemon 1.1-6

Paul greets a specific household church in this letter, but I suspect
his hopes and vision were expansive enough to include small
churches that would be meeting in other homes in ensuing centuries.
Small communities of faith continue a 2000-year-old tradition today
as we live our faith in the Lord Jesus, offer grace to one another, and
seek the peace of God and Jesus.

To research and write this chapter, I invited contributions from
many wise SCC animators and accompaniers with whom I have
been in community or with whom I have worked during the last 30
years. Many contributors are my peers in the SCC networking organization Buena Vista; others participated in the two international
SCC consultations that the Kellogg Institute at the University of
Notre Dame has sponsored. Their experience enriches the wisdom

this chapter offers about how to initiate the small Christian community process in the parish. "Community must be an active reality—not a concept," Paul O'Bryan cautions, speaking out of his experience as Pastoral Planning Coordinator for the Diocese of Maitland, Newcastle, Australia. What are some of the practical realities of introducing small communities in a parish?

Designing a Process

Many people who want to start a small Christian community will find help for designing their process in their diocesan offices. Those who find their dioceses have no office to offer guidance and resources can consult with national SCC organizations or other diocesan offices that do provide SCC resources. Some national organizations work with individual parishes; others prefer to link with a group of neighboring parishes or an entire diocese at one time. Most of these organizations offer resource materials, gatherings, and peer support for beginning or long-term small Christian communities. Consult the *Appendix* for the names and brief explanations of these SCC ministries.

Many people with the goal of starting SCCs prefer to devise their own start-up process. They may read materials and connect with SCC members in other parishes; then shape their findings into a process that suits their needs.

When the Parish Community of the Blessed Sacrament in Scottsdale, Arizona, decided to form SCCs in 1995, they planned carefully to introduce the concept to the parish at large. Deacon Dick Hoyet describes the process:

We did our homework for months, following up on leads, talking to folks across the country, and investigating resources that are available. What we learned was invaluable. Most importantly, we were reminded that SCCs grow slowly and it is quality, not quantity, that we are aiming for.

Blessed Sacrament dedicated one Sunday to SCCs with the

*homily and prayers of the faithful focusing on small communi-
ties and with a hospitality time after Mass with coffee, donuts,
SCC displays, and presentations. A few weeks later we sponsored a Sign-up Sunday for Lenten small groups. The intention
was that these Lenten groups would be a solid beginning of a
parish-wide small Christian community approach for the
parish.*[1]

Eight years later the small groups are still a focus for the parish.
SCC chaplain Deacon Clem Czapinski explains, "The small group
experience permeates the parish and plays an important role in ministries such as stewardship and truth and justice. We advertise regularly for new members and small communities are still mentioned in
prayers of the faithful each weekend. We're still plugging away."

The small community process can't evolve on a predictable time-
line. A parish needs to generate its best plans but also respond to
events that happen and move with the energy of the people who
come forward. How and when a parish group put its process into
place will depend upon:

> ➤ the past experience of parishioners with the concept of faith
>   sharing; for example, a parish that has participated in
>   RENEW can build on that experience;

> ➤ the support the pastor, pastoral council, and staff give small
>   Christian communities;

> ➤ the size of your parish, the parish calendar, and the number
>   of ministries involved. In a large, bustling parish folks may
>   think the program calendar has no room for more; however,
>   if the ministries aren't directly feeding parishioners' spiritual
>   hungers, many may welcome small Christian communities.

Animators and Accompaniers

For SCCS to take hold, individuals or small groups have to pass
on the vision for SCCs that hooked them into their possibilities.
When a growing number of parishioners understand the SCC vision
and spread their understanding, they will affect the whole parish.

Who needs to catch the vision? Each parish needs at least three kinds of support.

VISION CATCHERS 1: Pastors, staff persons, pastoral council members, ministry leaders and other parish leaders will need to understand what the SCC process aims to accomplish.
These people may not be the core accompaniers or animators in the parish, but they are invaluable as *promoters* and *supporters*.

SCC animators and accompaniers in parishes new to the concept of small Christian communities need to take time to listen to the different unmet spiritual needs, ideas, and possibilities that people in the parish can articulate. This means meeting with the pastoral council, staff people, and leaders of existing organizations, so that everyone feels included in the process of making small groups work in the parish. It involves working closely with the faith formation staff and volunteers and especially those responsible for RCIA. Only in the rarest circumstances are small Christian communities a total substitute for other types of religious education for children or adults. This listening will help synchronize and integrate efforts, so the new model doesn't threaten anyone and together the efforts of all result in comprehensive faith formation.

VISION CATCHERS 2: A core community of staff and volunteers who thoroughly understand the vision of SCC will be the key planners of the parish small-group experience and accompany the groups with ongoing support.
Forming one small group—a core community—is one way to start small Christian communities in a parish. This core group will do small Christian community and explore the SCC vision simultaneously. Ultimately members of this core team will accompany and offer peer support to other groups.

Personal experience with small Christian community is vital for core staff and volunteer members. Rosemary Bleuher, Associate Director for Adult Faith and Small Community Formation in the Diocese of Joliet, explains, "I had just completed a Masters in

Community and Organizational Development, which was beneficial for the organizing part of my job. But I needed the experience of being part of an SCC to know what it was I was aiming for. I learned through the years of being a member of an SCC."

Like Rosemary, the core community members need personal experience of what they are aiming for before they begin to introduce small groups to the parish at large. Experience is as important as theory in preparing to accompany other communities credibly.

Core members may come from any parish groups that already engage in faith sharing. Perhaps some of the baptized have continued gathering after completing their initiation through RCIA into the Church. In parishes that have worked with the RENEW program, one or two groups may continue to meet. A prayer group, mothers' group, or seniors' group may have many characteristics of a small Christian community outlined in chapter one. Some people from such groups may embrace the SCC vision and welcome participation in a core community. At the outset members of the core group must spend time coming to a common understanding of what they are aiming for and agree about the kind of communities they will nurture in the parish.

In a parish with little small-group activity, an accompanier can invite 10-15 potentially interested and committed folks to begin gathering on a regular basis. Attracting these participants can happen by word of mouth, advertising in the church bulletin, and asking parish leaders for their suggestions. A core team should reflect parish diversity and will benefit from variety. It is wise to invite young and old, women and men, timid and bold, doers and thinkers, parish leaders and back-pew sitters, newcomers and life-long parishioners.

Building up this core small community takes patience. Think long term for this initial small group. Plan to gather weekly or bi-weekly for six months to a year as a small group before planning to launch other groups. Just be. Experience the community that you hope lots of others will soon be doing. Be open to the Spirit who will be in charge. Expect the unexpected. Be willing to adjust, modify, and fine tune the way the group does things. Be prepared for some folks to drop out because the group isn't what they expected. Be open to new members who hear about what you are doing and want to join.

Before people join the core team, most will need assurance that they will have the chance to evaluate their experience of participating and are not making a lifelong commitment to ministry as a core-group member. But be honest that you hope they will catch the spirit and help out however they can for a couple of years at least. Participants need to know they are forming a special kind of small Christian community, one that is also taking on the task of a ministry in the parish. Some parishes have tried forming an initial small group with the intention of each person or couple in the group going their own way after a year to animate a new community. This can backfire—worse-case scenario: the group members decline to move on to other groups. At best, it is stressful for a group to bond only to go their separate ways.

Eventually some core community members will choose to move on for whatever reason. Core team members can add the challenge of people leaving and joining the team to their list of personal experiences that will help them accompany other small communities. Ultimately, after a number of years, a core group can call new members from the communities that have formed in the parish. This will give many folks the opportunity to participate for a time in the ministry of small Christian community accompanier as well as continue as members of their own small groups.

At Spirit of Christ Catholic Community in Arvada, Colorado, staff person Barbara Howard and a large group of volunteers accompany some 60 SCCs. "I love working with the Core Team," says Barbara. "They are committed, creative, and vocal. The ideas they raise, discuss, sometimes discard, and most often implement come from their faith in Jesus, the heart of their experience in the SCCs, and their commitment to parish. They help me from getting too subjective and repetitive in doing the ministry of SCC invitation and support."

Core team members at Spirit of Christ value attending to details. "The big vision rests on taking care of details in recruiting, sign-up, group assignments, materials." The team relies on their staff person "for what the parish plans for the future, for knowing parish culture and whose toes not to step on, for getting out a newsletter for the SCCs." The responsibilities of accompaniers (including staff) can include:

➤ Passing on the vision through parish newsletter stories, bulletin announcements, and pulpit time;

➤ Signing up participants and forming groups;

➤ Designing a database to track small groups;

➤ Training animators and facilitators for the groups;

➤ Choosing and/or suggesting small-group resources;

➤ Accompanying the groups, offering support, heightening awareness of the SCC vision, and keeping the groups connected with each other and the parish.

Accompaniers can accomplish these responsibilities by—

➤ Planning retreats, bringing in speakers, and hosting large-group gatherings of animators or all members of the small groups;

➤ Producing a newsletter for small-group members;

➤ Offering to visit small groups as a peer supporter and connector;

➤ Continuing to expand their own vision by reading, attending local or national gatherings of SCC folks;

➤ Nurturing their own faith life and making the SCC experience a priority in their own lives.

Where parishes have no staff person for small communities to rely on, core teams can ask the pastor to meet regularly with their all-volunteer group to facilitate an official link between the small communities and the parish at large. All-volunteer core groups can get support from diocesan resource personnel and/or from books, newsletters and other publications, from national organizations and by attending convocations of small Christian communities. (See *Appendix.*)

VISION CATCHERS 3: Small-group animators catch the vision and bring it to life within the individual groups.

The animator is the person(s) whose responsibility it is to learn about and appreciate the vision of small Christian communities, who nurtures that vision in a particular small group, who connects the group to the larger church, and who coordinates activities of the group. This book reserves the term *facilitator* for those who guide a particular faith-sharing session of the group. At times one person serves both capacities, but the animator need not facilitate, nor is this dual role preferred.

Small-group animators are the heart of the small Christian community experience. They are not leaders set apart from the others in the group. Australian theologian and author Paul O'Bryan borrows the term "one-anothering" to describe the role for animators.

> *Animators and, eventually, all members of the community are called to build up or create the communal life of the Small Church Community by drawing upon and developing the gifts of all members of the community. Thus, the creative presence of God that exists in the community through the Holy Spirit and which is ministered in the community through a one-anothering process that seeks to draw all members of the community to their "full potential" and to "fullness of life." The learning processes, the personal growth, the building of self esteem, and the development of gifts and skills are all concrete ways that the creative activity of God is at work in the SCC.*
>
> *At the same time, members of the community are called to minister the salvific presence of God to one-another and to help free one another from the "burdens" that weigh people down. All people are sinful and each in their own way carry*

the burdens of failure, of sorrow and guilt, of grief, of depression, of a poor self image and a lack of confidence, of illness or disability, or a lack of hope.

Through the personal qualities of care and support, compassion and forgiveness, attentive listening, empathy and sympathy, encouragement, and challenge, members of the small church community, especially the animators, enflesh the saving activity of God by "walking with" the other or "helping to free" other members of the community from the burdens that they carry.

In this way, the one-anothering process is both creative and salvific. It is in this way, that the salvation of God becomes a real thing in people's lives.

This one-anothering concept assumes a key objective—that everyone will take responsibility for the group. This means that anyone who wishes will eventually feel comfortable facilitating sessions, representing the group in the parish, and even taking on the role of animator.

Training for small-group animators will lead them on a path similar to that of accompaniers, perhaps not in such depth or before they begin to gather with a group. Basic awareness of the vision of small Christian communities is a priority. Animators need to recognize that a SCC is not a prayer group, not a ministry group, not a bible-study group, not a social group, and not a support group, although a healthy SCC will include some characteristics of each. They will understand that small Christian communities create the unique experience of faith sharing. With on-going formation small-group animators (and accompaniers) can develop and update their skills in conflict resolution, building group identity, group decision-making, and evaluation.

In *Small Christian Communities: Visions and Practicalities,* author James O'Halloran, SDB, suggests a team of three animators for each group so that should one be missing, the other two can carry on. He also lists critical qualities and skills that animators and other group members should nurture in themselves:

➤ empathy (the ability of listening to and walking with another);

➤ an openness to the other;

➤ responsible, creative, non-menacing, non-defensive challenge to difficult situations;

➤ readiness to deal with conflict promptly;

➤ acceptance of diversity.[2]

Based on their work with New Way of Being Church in Britain and their extensive travels in Latin America and Africa, Jeanne Hinton and Peter B. Price outline two additional ministries they see as important to small groups.

In New Way workshops we appoint timekeepers whose job it is to remind those of us who go on a bit that time is almost up...Agreeing to a simple ground rule that one person will watch the time and help others to do the same makes all the difference. (They also appoint someone to be responsible for) keeping a memory of meetings and events... an important tool of community development. Keeping and recalling the memory provides a broad overall perspective. It is an encouragement in hard times and a call to ongoing commitment in easier times.[3]

In my own small community, The Oilers, some of our most important bonding times flowed from bringing out the photos or video tapes, reminiscing about past times together, and recalling who we are as a group.

Other responsibilities for the small-group animator include practical considerations such as organizing meeting calendars and being aware of the special needs of group members. One handy service an animator can provide is assembling a current list of members' names and contact information. Animators can share this list with the parish core team.

What Groups Do When They Gather

Finding Resources

Using any materials designed especially for small Christian communities is a good way for groups to begin. These booklets and pamphlets lay out a well-balanced session that the facilitator and others in the group can easily follow without a lot of small group experience or preparation. In its *Resource Page* and *Resource Book*, Buena Vista makes a clear distinction between materials intended specifically for SCCs and other materials that will require more advanced facilitation skills. In *Come As You Are*, the NAPRC has developed a quality resource expressly for newly-forming communities that extends the initial invitation to community and is easy to use.

In some parishes the pastor, a staff person, and/or the core group chooses one resource for all small groups to use. For newly-forming groups this works quite well. But eventually, as initial groups mature and new ones continue to form, parishes and core teams need to offer a variety and choice of materials. The parish library at St. William's in Naples, Florida, sets aside one area especially for samples of resources for small groups. Some parishes purchase 15 or more copies of especially good resources that groups can borrow. Some well-established SCCs may wish to peruse publishers' catalogs and bookstore shelves on their own to find just the right material.

Scripture is one good focus for small groups of all kinds. It presents inexhaustible opportunities for faith sharing and prayer and, because of its universality, serves as an important way to connect with the larger Church community. Personally, I am less distracted during celebration of the word on Sunday when I have recently spent some time with a group considering what the readings say to me in light of my own life experiences. I greet the proclamation of the gospel with familiarity and greater anticipation. Some resources build reflection and life questions around the Church's lectionary, its cycles of scripture readings for Sunday worship. The term *lectionary-based* identifies these resources.

I suggest lectionary-based materials for new small groups for reasons besides readying us to hear the Sunday gospel. First, several excellent resources lay out an entire small-group session that is easy for beginning facilitators to use, including prayer, scripture reflection, faith-sharing questions, and invitations to the work of charity and justice. Bernard Lee's study of small Christian communities identified *Sunday by Sunday* from Good Ground Press and *Quest* from the Diocese of Hartford as the two most-used lectionary-based resources in SCCs. Second, the lectionary offers an easy way to extend faith sharing throughout the parish, to connect the experience of SCCs with each other, and coordinate a unified, parish-wide encounter with the word beyond Sunday liturgy. For example, the pastor can utilize the material as homily review. Ministry committees and families can use parts of the reflection, a question, and prayer to open a committee meeting or at the dinner table. Some SCCs focus exclusively on the lectionary; others focus on the Sunday gospel to begin and go on to other themes and topics. Extending the use of lectionary-based resources can bring more parishioners to Sunday worship prepared to hear, absorb, and live God's word. Of course, prayer, church documents, social justice, church history, and other topics can serve equally well as topics for small Christian communities.

The Priority of Faith Sharing

Small groups for faith sharing differ from bible-study groups or prayer groups in one important way—they aim to reflect on their lives. Recognizing this difference is a priority for SCC accompaniers, animators, facilitators, and members. Like bible study, small Christian communities reflect on scripture. The practice of faith sharing, however, leads adults beyond learning what scripture communicates to consider our own life experience in light of the scripture message and current events. Faith sharing reaches beyond information to transformation of individuals, the community, and the world. The process of faith sharing is theological reflection.

Although this term sounds intimidating, it merely means reflection on God and the things of God, something we all do.

One member of St. Anthony's small Christian community, St. Gregory's Parish, Maryville, Missouri, said she had been a lector since women could serve in that ministry but until she participated in a small Christian community she never understood what the scriptures meant.[4]

Effective faith-sharing questions differ from bible-study discussion starters in that they encourage personal experience rather than facts or theories. The practice of theological reflection does not involve right and wrong answers, rather people share personal experiences that help connect our lives to God. For example, a bible study of the scripture passage that begins this chapter might focus on when the letter was written, who Philemon was, and what Paul's relationship to Philemon was. A small Christian community will focus on questions that evoke faith sharing, such as: "Paul did a good job of affirming Philemon's faith. How is your faith affirmed? Who, besides the members of this group, encourages you in your faith? What are you doing to affirm the faith of others?"

All life is gift and sacrament of God's presence. Our daily lives and the daily news in our world are potential sources for faith sharing. Faith sharing sharpens our awareness of the Spirit's stirrings in our everyday lives. In *Re-gather the Parish: A Newsletter of the Melbourne SCC Network*, a contributor suggests "learning the sacramentality of daily life by asking questions such as:

➤ What surprises me about this event, action, object?

➤ What does this remind me of? Why?

➤ How does this connect with my faith?

➤ What will I now do differently?"

Felicia Wolf, OSF, accompanies small Christian communities and helps people learn to facilitate groups. She reflects on the process of faith sharing and theological reflection.

The process of life is to become who God made us to be. This process never ends, not even with death. It is also a natural process, something we do all the time. However, to cooperate more fully with God, we need to reflect on this process in a deliberate, conscious way. Theologians of our time call this process theological reflection.

First we need to know who we think we are so that we have a point of view. We do this by taking account of our life in order to find the themes and patterns that make up our biographical point of view.

Once we have this point of view we go to our Wisdom Tradition, which is the finished earthly life of Jesus and the unfinished resurrected life of Jesus as told to us by early church fathers all the way up to the songs we sing at Mass and the homily. By doing this we develop what we understand as our church's view of Jesus' life.

We never complete either phase. The points of view we develop are our best guess for right now. Next week it might be expanded and enriched. That is why we need to continue this process through our life.

Once we understand these points of view, we ask, "How does Jesus' life affect my (our) life? And how does my (our) life affect Jesus' resurrected life?"

We can stop the process right here. The answers to the above questions can keep us busy for a long time. However, once we become comfortable with this dialogue between Jesus' life and the life of our community, we can go on to ask about the life of the secular world.

What are the life stories of the present era? What do current events say about our stage of life? What does the secular world say about Jesus? We need to ask ourselves, then, how do our stories in Jesus affect the present era and how does the present era affect our life in Jesus?

From this dialogue with the secular world, we gain new understandings of who we are and what we must do. If the

spirit is willing and our wills strong, we will do what we must
to carry on our life in Jesus, who is "the way the truth and
the light." [5]

The Essentials of Church

Small Christian communities are conscientious about including
all the essentials of church. Besides nurturing community and
reflecting on scripture, these essentials include prayer and service
and justice. Good resource materials written to help SCCs understand and include all of these essentials.

Cormac Murphy-O'Connor, Cardinal Archbishop of Westminster,
describes how the experience of small Christian communities connects these essentials.

> *The influence of the Church on our culture is most tangibly felt*
> *through the actual witness of the people of God. The authen-*
> *ticity and effectiveness of that witness is in turn dependent, at*
> *least in part, on our continuing to grow and mature as people*
> *of deep spirituality and holiness. Within smaller groups, where*
> *a greater degree of trust and confidence can be built up, people*
> *are encouraged and inspired to go further and deeper on their*
> *journey of faith than they might otherwise. People begin to*
> *discover, and then to share more openly, their relationship with*
> *God, with each other, with the whole of creation. Out of these*
> *kinds of reflection a greater conviction of the importance of*
> *putting faith into action can develop. Justice and peace issues*
> *take on added urgency and significance. So, too, can a desire*
> *to become more closely involved in the liturgy, in youth work,*
> *in catechetics and in other aspects of the pastoral, spiritual*
> *and social life of the Church.* [6]

Social Time

Enjoying each other's company is vital in small communities and
needs a significant time set aside in every gathering. This can simply mean sharing coffee and cookies for half an hour after the faith-

sharing session. Or it can mean potluck dinners before faith sharing begins. Many groups regularly schedule parties that include nonparticipating spouses and children. Others go on summer camping or hiking trips together. Social time bonds the members of a group as much as prayer, faith sharing, and support of one another in difficult times. *Luz y Esperanza* (Light and Hope) SCC, Diocese of Santiago, Chile, feels that their most special times are "when there is a celebration and we end singing and eating roasted chicken with salads. It is a gathering when everybody cooks."[7]

Upwey SCC of Belgrave Parish in the Melbourne Archdiocese in Australia describes their community succinctly:

When we gather on a fortnightly basis, we share what has been happening in our lives. We pray the Scriptures and share our faith and insights. We pray together for one another and for others in need. We support the missionary work of a Salesian priest, Father Hans, in Pakistan. On one occasion we shared the Lenten scriptures with a group from the local Uniting Church. From time to time our current parish priest, Father Brian, joins us and we have a home Mass and then a meal. We laugh, cry, and encourage one another. Jokes are shared on the e-mail. Crossword clues are discussed and thrashed over. Many are interested in sports, the theatre, cinema and the creative arts. We conclude each meeting with supper and hugs and good-bye.[8]

Configuration of Groups

Traditional SCCs include a variety of folks to reflect the membership of the larger church. Sign-up sheets often include a choice of days of the week and times of the day (morning, afternoon, evening) when participants are available. This usually generates a good mix of age, gender, and background. The *InTouch Newsletter* from St. John the Evangelist Parish in Columbia, Maryland, describes the variety in their SCCs.

"Extroverted," "energetic," and "pragmatic" were the adjectives chosen by B. J. Marshall (to describe his East Coast suburban group). He sees the age range, between 24 and 70, of men and women, married and single, "a nice dichotomy," saying that the young consider themselves invincible and the older members "love us enough to let us fail."

Affinity Groups

For myriad reasons, some people choose to gather in groups alike in age, gender, special populations, or culture. These groups can also gather successfully within parishes. Carol Blank, service team member at St. John's, calls these SCCs in her parish by the term *affinity groups*.

The decision to actively promote affinity groups grew from a small but constant number of requests over the years and from two recent positive experiences with the concept.

The first was the service team's (core group) effort to help a man find other men who would like to form an SCC. With a few personal contacts and a notice in the parish bulletin, several interested parishioners came together and began meeting. The second experience began with one parishioner's desire to form an Asian group. She and her husband first contacted another Asian couple. They suggested others who would be compatible, though they were not of Asian descent. The "Asian" group—with members of several races—meets happily today.

The affinity groups, like our randomly formed SCCs, will be structured around the basic elements of church: community, prayer, scripture, and service. The service team will coordinate formation of new groups primarily on the basis of sign-ups received on focus weekends.

Affinity groups that have been suggested are listed below and are included on the sign-up forms, which also have space for write-ins.

Solo on Sunday
Interfaith couples
Groups based in a particular culture or language
Gays and lesbians and their friends and families
Parents of teens
Living single
Young mothers.

Family Small Christian Communities

More and more SCCs try to include all ages and family members in some significant way. This helps build community, bonds members and families, and gives children a well-rounded experience of church beyond Sunday Mass and religious education classes. Some communities plan social events for the entire family at regularly scheduled intervals. Others include children in every get-together but split up for faith sharing for different age groups. Still others, like the Holy Chaos SCC in Pleasanton, California, are a truly intergenerational community. Amy Sluss describes their community.

It includes 14 adults and the children of 12 of those adults. The 18 children range in age from 4 years to 15 years of age. The children are included in virtually all of the activities of the community, including prayer and scripture reflection. They are connected to their parish through a staff person.

Each family is responsible for facilitating at least one gathering during the year including researching and presenting the topic. Together and individually they are involved in social ministry and are working toward more involvement in justice issues.

Most of the families live far away from extended families. Small Christian community often substitutes for aunts, uncles and cousins that we are missing. [9]

Introducing Small Groups Parish Wide

St. John Evangelist Parish in Columbia, Maryland, has an active small Christian community ministry. Patricia Barbernitz, Pastoral Associate for Evangelization, describes the experience in their parish of the whole process of starting small Christian communities.

> *Beginning new groups is always an adventure. They usually begin with a series of sign-up forms, grouped together by a check mark under the same day of the week. Someone from among that number agrees to take on some leadership in getting the group started.*
>
> *Usually that is a somewhat reluctant agreement, but that person accepts the list of phone numbers and begins the initial calls. Then, there is the round of "phone tag" and the people who have changed their minds.*
>
> *Finally there is a first meeting with its decisions about where to meet, what materials to use, how to recruit enough other members to reach a viable size for a group, and discovering who is who and where do I belong in this group. Beginning involves energy, hard work, and risk.*
>
> *The next step is easier; it often comes as a surprise. Suddenly the group begins to use words like "us," "our group," and "isn't it amazing how we all got together with just the right people?" The reluctant pastoral leader (animator) also finds all the help needed to keep the group moving together: others make reminder calls, plan for prayer, provide refreshments, take turns facilitating sessions. A SCC has been formed in the grace of the Holy Spirit.[10]*

One significant decision facing core communities as they plan toward initiating new small groups is how to choose animators and how to train them. Options run the gamut. Some parishes call forth animators and train them in the parish vision of SCCs and small-group dynamics before inviting the parish at large to consider joining SCCs. Other parishes, like St. John the Evangelist, rely on animators arising serendipitously when the parish offers the opportunity to join a community. In this case the "training" of animators occurs over time through workshops, retreats, newsletters, and SCC visitations.

One or two sessions with folks who answer the call to animate a group seems the minimum necessary to pass along the initial vision, clarify expectations of the role, and explain the support offered by the core group of accompaniers. The pastoral team from the Archdiocese of Seattle has developed a valuable and extensive package for those who choose an in-depth training for facilitators and animators. (See *Appendix*.)

The notion of small groups will be totally new to some people who hear a parish's call to community. They will want to know what they are being invited to join and why they should accept the call. An invitation needs to be gentle enough not to be intimidating, clear enough to let people know what they will be getting into, and enthusiastic enough to entice busy people to consider adding one more notation to their calendars. Long-term commitment has to grow out of the experience of community.

In my own case, if someone had told me in 1971 I was embarking on a lifelong adventure, I would probably have passed when I heard the call to community. As it was, community was allowed to grow in me in response to the Spirit's own timetable and plan for me and my family. I described my experience in *Buena Vista Ink*:

> *I had two toddlers in two high chairs, feeding them their dinner while I made sense of the remains of a weekly grocery shopping trip. Rusty was in the garage under the '64 Fairlane addressing yet another obstacle to reliable transportation. And then this PRIEST was knocking at our door. What was he doing at our home?*
>
> *There was nothing to do but let him in.*
>
> *He delivered a spoonful of soup to a small, hungry mouth and asked which cupboard the bag of sugar belonged in! Soon he was on his back on the floor of the garage, handing Rusty the tools he needed and offering mechanical advice. When all was in some semblance of order he sprang it on us. "How*

*would you like to meet the other Catholics in your neighbor-
hood?" Crafty devil! After all this how could we say no?*

*Meeting those neighboring Catholics was the beginning of a
lifetime experience of small community. The challenge to
interact with others in this way introduced me to another way
to be church."[11]*

Prior to a SCC sign-up weekend, the core team or SCC staff person needs to prepare the parish through bulletin announcements, stories in the parish newsletter, and the pastor's support for SCCs from
the pulpit. Some parishes even design a SCC brochure to give or
send to every parishioner.

Showing one of the several excellent, basic videos about SCCs
between Masses for one or two weeks can stimulate interest among
parishioners. These videos are especially good to help folks understand that small Christian communities are a Church-wide phenomenon. I was surprised to learn after more than 15 years in a parish
founded on the concept of and focusing on the experience of SCCs
that some members thought it was an experience exclusive to that
parish.

On the sign-up weekend(s) I suggest:

➤ Folks in charge of sign-up tables need to be accompaniers or
animators with a proficient understanding of the vision of
SCCs and the particular efforts in the parish. They will be
ready with credible answers to inevitable questions.

➤ Individual cards for each parishioner to fill out including
space for all necessary contact information as well as criteria
the core team has identified for forming groups (times
available, special needs).

➤ Leave a space for special information on the sign-up card.
If someone has particular background in small groups or
scripture or can offer some other particular skill, this is the
time to find out. I suggest not being too specific. Let the
Holy Spirit uncover talents the team would never have
thought to ask for!

➤ Combine sign up with coffee and donuts to encourage more time for folks to consider the opportunity.

One very important practical piece of advice: Prepare a database ahead of time to keep track of those who sign up. Keying in information from all the sign-up sheets may seem like a waste of time but hand sorting cards into viable groups is an overwhelming task. This information is useful to have at your fingertips. Several inexpensive programs provide formats for entering names, addresses, phone number(s), email addresses, day and time of availability, and other pertinent information. As SCCs develop, add fields for the name of animator(s), conferences, or special training the person has attended. An especially ambitious core group can even track the resource materials each group has used and their evaluation of the material for other groups to read. If no one in your core group is database literate, let the parish know of your need through a bulletin announcement or ask a teenager!

Plan to spend time sorting participants' information and forming communities immediately following sign-up weekend(s). If potential participants sign up but hear nothing for several weeks, they will feel discouraged. Interest will wane.

Many have successfully initiated long-term groups by starting with short-term commitments. At the end of Lenten groups, for instance, invite participants to continue. Leave time for discernment about a longer-term commitment. Don't put folks on the spot by asking the animators to issue an invitation unexpectedly within the group. Perhaps a letter sent jointly from the core community and the animator. Not everyone in a group will accept the invitation to form a SCC, so a core team must anticipate juggling to combine smaller groups. Reorganized groups are new communities. Just as any time someone leaves or joins a group, these new communities will need to begin at the beginning and nurture a new group identity.

Keeping the Vision Alive

Once is not enough to form SCCs in a parish. The core team or community can decide how often to form new groups. Most parishes do this on a yearly basis. One good time to start new groups is in the fall. Fall is a time of renewal and new energy; many activities follow the school year and parish/church is no exception. Groups can meet for regular faith-sharing sessions September through May and reserve the summer months for more relaxed, social gatherings. I caution against eliminating summer gatherings all together as it is often hard to resume in the fall unless the group is a very committed, bonded small Christian community. Lent is also a traditional time to offer beginning group sign-ups because folks are often looking for an intensely spiritual experience during this time.

Annual or semi-annual large group events for all members of all small groups are ideal opportunities for spiritual retreat, ongoing adult formation, and reflection on the vision of small church. This is a perfect opportunity to connect the groups to one another and the larger Church by showing a short video followed by small-group time or by bringing in a captivating speaker to re-energize communities. Invite the pastor to say a few words, offering his support for SCC efforts.

Create a presence for the small communities in the parish. Marketing is necessary to promote spiritual enrichment processes. Buena Vista sells inexpensive ribbons for small community members to wear at parish events printed with the suggestion to "Ask me about my small Christian community!"

Small Christian communities need their own identity. At some point, kick off a community-naming process. After groups have chosen a name ask them to make a small banner for their group. Have a potluck dinner for the groups to display the banners and explain their choice of a name. Encourage the groups to use the banner as a prayer focus during their gatherings along with a lighted candle, an open bible, and perhaps a small world globe to remind them of the universal Church of which they are an integral part.

Although small groups are not the available workforce for the parish, carefully chosen parish events, such as a pancake breakfast sponsored by the groups, is a good way to create recognition and pique interest of non-group members. Or, the small groups can take responsibility for one booth at the parish picnic. It can display groups' banners to grab attention.

Encourage small group members to attend a local or national conference for small Christian communities. Perhaps the parish budget can help with expenses. Participants will return with new insights and fresh enthusiasm. Ask them to write a story about what they learned and print it in the parish or SCC newsletter. Or maybe they can tell about their experience at a large-group community gathering.

Suggest that SCCs join the small Christian community international twinning program. In this way they will be linked with a community in a different country or culture in mutual sharing of daily life, spiritual encouragement, and prayer. This is another excellent way for SCCs to understand their valuable place in the global Church.

Finally, it is crucial to keep your parish small groups for faith sharing and small Christian communities connected to others. Join one or another national organization listed in the *Appendix*. Subscribe to one or more of the excellent SCC newsletters published globally. None of us can do it all alone. Remember this is all about one-anothering in the same way that the earliest Christians practiced mutual love and service. With the ease of contemporary national and international travel and communication, we don't have to wait for St. Paul to come to us. We have a unique and precious opportunity to share one on one with other Christians and make Church a daily experience.

Summing Up Practical Suggestions

➤ The structure has to work for the people, not the people for the structure.

➤ Start from where you are; build on existing possibilities in the parish and neighborhood.

➤ A core group of people immerses themselves in the vision and experience of small Christian community and then accompanies new groups as they begin to do the same.

➤ Animators and eventually all members of the community are called to build up or create the communal life of the small church community.

➤ Keep the vision alive by continuing the process: pray, listen, be patient, discern, animate, invite; pray, listen, be patient, discern, animate, invite; pray, listen, be patient, discern, animate, invite!

PRAYER

Holy Spirit, light the fire of community in us.
God of Wisdom, enrich our minds, hearts, and souls
that your will, not ours, be done.
God of Patience, be with us as we work toward true community
ourselves and generate community among others.
God of Strength, hold us in your agile fingers
that we may be resilient and resourceful.
God of Compassion, sustain us
that we may be warmth, blessing, and gracious welcome for all.
God of Wonder, let us not forget the joy in our ministry;
remind us to dance as we work,
to dream our noblest dreams,
and to thrill at your nearness. Amen

Endnotes

[1] Dick Hoyet, *Buena Vista Ink*, January, 1997.

[2] James O'Halloran, SDB, *Small Christian Communities: Visions and Practicalities* (Dublin: Columba Press, 2003).

[3] Jeanne Hinton and Peter B. Price, *Changing Communities: Church From the Grassroots* (London: CTBI Publications, 2003) 33.

[4] Robert Pelton, Nancy Reissner, Barbara Darling, eds., "Global Small Christian Community Research Project: Latin American/North American Church Concerns" University of Notre Dame and the Center for Mission Research and Study at Maryknoll, 2002. Access this research at: www.buenavista.org.

[5] Felicia Wolf, a reflection on John Dunne, CSC, *A Search for God in Time and Memory* (Sheldon Press, 1975).

[6] Cormac Murphy-O'Connor, *Tablet*: May 31, 2003.

[7] Pelton, Reissner, and Darling, *Op. Cit.*

[8] *Ibid.*

[9] See Amy Sluss, *Family Faith Communities: 10 Ready-to-Use Family Gatherings* (St. Paul, Minnesota: Good Ground Press, 2003).

[10] Pat Barbernitz, *InTouch SCC Newsletter*, St. John the Evangelist Parish, Columbia, MD.

[11] Barbara Darling, *Buena Vista Ink*, November, 1995.

CHAPTER THREE

Initiating Non-Parish Communities of Faith

by Jack Ventura, SM

The First Small Faith Community

In the story of the Visitation (Luke 1:39-56), Luke paints a beautiful story of an encounter between two women. For many people, this gospel account of the visit of the young Mary to her older cousin Elizabeth is a symbol of mission and service. While I believe that is true (two people caring for each other is a great lesson for all of us), I would like to suggest another interpretation, especially for those interested in the creation and development of small communities of faith (SFC).

If we sit with this story for a short time, we can see something very powerful is happening for these two women. God has burst into their lives in ways they don't fully understand. A woman who is past childbearing years is suddenly with child. On the other end of the lifeline, a young woman whose life cycles are just starting is also with child. Both Mary and Elizabeth must have been surprised, delighted, confused, and maybe even scared. They might have even felt alone in their experience. In Mary's bewilderment, her first response is to go to Elizabeth—not necessarily to care for Elizabeth, but rather to share her experience with another person who also has been changed because of God's entry into her life. In other words, Mary acts; she sets out in haste for Elizabeth's house (Luke 1:39). She invites; she enters Elizabeth's house and greets her (Luke 1:40). She shares; she lets Elizabeth know what's happening in her life (Luke 1:41-45). She prays, "My soul magnifies the Lord" (Luke 1:46-55) and stays with Elizabeth for three months (Luke 1:56).

These two women with their unborn babies enter into a faith-sharing community. One woman was shunned for her lack of pregnancy; the other was ashamed because she had no husband. Because they were marginalized, of the same gender, related by blood and didn't belong to a parish community, the story of the Visitation can be a foundation for those seeking to start a small community of faith outside the parish setting.

Small communities of faith are becoming a reality for many parishes in the United States. As parishes struggle to deal with the challenges of time, treasure, talent, and personnel, some pastors and bishops are seeing the great value and biblical context of forming a parish into small communities of faith. The United States and the Catholic Church in the United States are much more pluralistic than when they were founded. The face of American small communities of faith mirrors this deep and treasured value—diversity in union. There is great diversity within the small community movement in America.

As I continue ministry with people in our Church, I realize how the yearning for a more fulfilled faith life comes to the surface of one's life at various stages of development. Some psychologists may call it personality growth, but I call it God's calling forth of vocation. This calling goes beyond the boundaries of parishes and parish-based small communities. It is diverse in gender, age, lifestyle, and purpose for gathering.

There are many reasons why people come together in faith. I would never try to make a list of all existing small communities of faith, but I have come across four types that are worth mentioning.

Four Examples of Small Communities of Faith

Religious Evangelical Community

The first is a *Religious Evangelical Community*, women and men who have been inspired by a particular vision and join together to live out the charism and spirituality of the founders of that group. They share a history and specific values and continue to add to the traditions of their ancestors, making an impact in the world today. Some examples are Franciscans, Sisters of St. Joseph, Christian Brothers, Sisters of Mercy, and of course my own religious community—the Society of Mary—the Marianists. The men and women who profess the evangelical counsels (vows) are essentially a small community of faith. Their life and faith gets nurtured within their local community or house. Together these small groups belong to the larger congregation and the worldwide church and society. Many of these groups do not find support within the parish structure. In addition, lay associates, lay affiliates, and former members may attach to the religious communities. These people have been called to live out the spirituality of the religious congregation as lay people. The spirit of the community, the founders, or the corporate ministry of the congregation may attract them. The groups may be mixed communities of lay and religious or religious only. These groups meet regularly, have a purpose and mission, support the members, and participate in many activities in society and Church. The religious congregation with its charism and spirituality is the common inspiration, not the parish.

Christian Family Community of Faith

Another broad-based experience is a *Christian Family Community of Faith*. These groups share a common experience, most often a retreat experience. They believe the family is the primary community of faith. The Marianist Christian Family Ministry has animated many small groups of families for years. The

Christian Family Movement is another existing organization. These groups gather and share the Word of God within the context of the lived experience of family. What is essential in this model is the importance and presence of children at gatherings. Many of these groups use a community model to pass on the faith to their children and may even receive the sacraments within this small community of faith. These groups cross parish boundaries, neighborhoods, towns, cities, and even states. They are geographically and culturally diverse. Development of faith life is their common purpose for gathering.

Ministry or Profession Faith Communities

Ministry or Profession Faith Communities are a growing model for another type of small community of faith. Again, these groups can be extremely diverse, including men and women, or be unisex. These people gather to explore the relationship of faith in a common workplace, stage of life, ministry, or social and ecclesial agenda. For many years, I belonged to a small community of vocation directors. When we gathered, we shared many experiences of our ministry in the context of the Word of God. They are different from support groups or professional associations because they are not task oriented. They have a shared vision; members find support for each other and have a public life and an external ministry. These groups might be those who gather within the same profession, a mothers' group, a men's group, a social justice community, or even small communities of students. Many schools have initiated a program of Christian Life Communities or Sodalities for their students, teachers, and administrators. For this model to work, the administration of the school must be committed and model a small community of faith. A high school in South Florida supports a model of faculty and staff who make a yearly public commitment during a Eucharist of the Holy Spirit at the beginning of the academic year. Depending on how some volunteer communities act, they are also a good example of these types of communities.

Marginalized Communities

The last model is *Marginalized Communities*. These people gather in small communities of faith because they stand on the margins of church and society. These groups do not feel connected or comfortable with parish and church structures for many reasons, which can include sexual orientation, gender, race, or age. These groups are very spiritual and see themselves within a social system. They challenge us to face the problems of exclusivity within the power structures of society and church. Many of these groups are ecumenical, are not lectionary based in their meetings, and see God as acting in their lives. For example, a spiritual center in Philadelphia, Pennsylvania, has as its mission to minister to those who are affected and infected with HIV/Aids. They support small communities of people who want to find God in the midst of the HIV/Aids epidemic. These small communities constantly ask, "How is God active within me and others?" As these communities of faith mature, members may become active in the mission and ministry of the spiritual center, involving the community in an outside public life. When marginalized communities develop, they help the larger community expand the frame of life. I believe these groups help us grow and change our assumptions.

Non-parish-based communities are a grassroots endeavor. Many of the members of these communities are just like Mary and Elizabeth, searching, probing, and sharing their lives. When God enters people's lives, they need to share and God is certainly entering people's lives today. Many other non-parish-based small communities of faith exist. Some are on the horizons, not yet fully formed. However they choose to describe themselves, the essential elements described in the beginning of this book are also components of these small communities of faith.

The Process of Forming a Non-Parish-Based, Small Faith Community

With the four types of non-parish-based communities as a backdrop, the next question becomes how to start one. In founding a small community of faith, the experience often begins with a deliberate effort. A sincere desire to find a small group in which to express and grow in faith may animate an individual. Someone who has experienced a small community may seek to found and animate another group. Others wait upon the Holy Spirit until they find, hear, witness, and observe another person who has been moved by the same Spirit express the need for such a group. A group of people feels the call to begin a small community and are not afraid to articulate those needs and desires with friends. They assemble a group through making contacts. The Holy Spirit inspires both the waiting and actively-inviting methods.

Who has the vision? Who has the call? Who has the need? These questions are most important in the formation of small faith communities—especially if they are to endure and be lifelong influences. Founders or animators of small faith communities, whether they are a single person or a group, strive to form communities that are inclusive, faith-filled, and relationship-oriented. To achieve results, the group must have a call and meet specific needs. Sometimes the call and the needs are mixed. Most people who are drawn to start a faith community are seeking "more life." At first, this may seem to be a vague desire. But the need expresses a call.

A founder or founders will have keen ears to hear statements such as, "There must be more to life than _____," or "I wish I could find a place where my faith can be _____," or "I wish I could be with people who share the same _____." Most of us can fill in the blanks with various words or expressions. Founders have the gift of listening and will respond in calling people together. Listening is the first step (after prayer) for the founder(s).

The next step is to search for others who have similar needs and convictions. In the story of the Visitation, Mary has a deep need to share her experience with the one person she knows will understand her story. She runs in haste to seek Elizabeth (Luke 1:39-40). The founding members of a small group must also have a need to develop and strengthen their faith or feel a call to begin a faith community. They will invite others who will also have a desire to live a particular spirituality or have interest in a common mission. The nucleus of this faith community may be only one or two people. However, over time the community will grow.

Prayer must accompany all steps of the process. Groups can begin because of the personality of a person or persons that want to begin a group. However, the group will not endure if the Holy Spirit is not involved. Paul's letters to the community of faith in Corinth pleads with them to be of the same mind and purpose rather than falling into factions according to who baptized whom (1 Corinthians 1:10-17). Faith communities are a work of the risen Christ and his Spirit, not the genius of humans. When we combine our human talents with the grace of God, we can accomplish great things.

In summary:

> Be or find a founder sensing a call from God to form a group, whether it is to meet faith needs or to be apostolic;

> Search out others who will find a home within the group— seek out seekers.

Identifying Founders, Animators

One successful method I have found in searching out founders is a very Marianist method—presence. This approach is very simple— attend many meetings, events, retreats, gatherings, and parties to observe and listen. When people express needs, try to respond by wondering with them and concretize how those needs might be met. At some point an individual or the group will dream of the beginnings of a SFC. Inviting others follows the dreaming. This method of developing a SFC is gentle and probing. It is not filled with badgering, pressing, pushing, or pressuring. Remember that your cooperation with God will provide the founding members. Like Mary, attempt to "Do whatever he tells us." Rely on the fact that Jesus' mission has not ended and that the Holy Spirit is alive and active in people's lives.

A Beginning Step-by-Step Approach

There is no one, right way to achieve the goal of founding a small community of any kind. Being flexible and committed to the process are the successful components in starting a new community. The following are some suggestions that I have developed in attempting to begin a new small community of faith.

STEP 1: Brainstorm perceived needs and assess what the Spirit is stirring in you. This first step presumes that you have been praying and listening to the perceived needs of people around you. You have a clear sense of something missing in your life. Make a list of your feelings, reactions, and the gaps in your life where God needs to enter.

STEP 2: Make a list of people who you think would like to invest in forming a small community of faith. After you list the needs of your soul, discern that list with people you know. Check it out with them and see if they have similar needs or desires. Ask them if they know others who are asking similar questions. Be specific—invite them to think about forming a small group. Also, ask them if they would invite someone they know.

STEP 3: Set a time, date, and place to have an investigative meeting. Once you have a list of people, invite them to an initial gathering. Remember this gathering is an inquiry session. Your goal is to gather people searching for more.

STEP 4: Set a time limit and be sure that is communicated to those you are inviting. The first gathering should not be any longer than two hours. People are busy and their time is valuable.

STEP 5: Invite by mail and follow-up by phone. Send a formal letter of invitation to the gathering. Be very specific about the purpose of the gathering. Also, mention there are no commitments at this time. All you are trying to accomplish at this step is to coordinate the "seekers." Some people may not be interested; some may be interested but may not be able to attend the gathering; and some may say, "I've been waiting for something like this."

STEP 6: Develop the gathering. Serve drinks and snacks. Although this may start as a social gathering, you have a specific goal in mind. You must be prepared for those who will be coming. It doesn't have to be a sophisticated meeting—just be prepared. An example follows:

> ➤ Welcome & opening prayer

> ➤ Introductions

> ➤ Stated purpose of gathering—to investigate the forming of a small faith community

> ➤ Allow for sharing of personal needs and expectations of the people gathered. Sometimes a small survey will help the introverts in the group.

> ➤ Are those who are gathered hearing similar desires and/or needs? Is there enough interest to start a small community? Is there enough interest to start several communities of faith? Is there a willingness to meet again?

> ➤ If yes, set the time, date, and place for the next gathering(s).

> ➤ Closing prayer

> ➤ Allow for some social time. You will gather more information during this time than in the actual meeting.

Ongoing Community

Once you have a commitment from others to enter the journey of starting a small community of faith, the next few gatherings must be fact finding in origin. What the community must decide upon are:

➤ When and where to meet

➤ Frequency of meetings

➤ Purpose of the gatherings

➤ Setting a philosophy and vision for the community

➤ Style of a typical meeting

➤ Defining the size of a community. What is too small? What is too big to be effective? (You can use the guidelines already listed in the beginning chapters of this book.)

➤ Expectations of the members

➤ Identity of the group—possibly in a written statement

➤ Organizational structure of the community

➤ Leadership

➤ Roles of the members

➤ Naming the community

➤ Owning the community

➤ Defining style of prayer

➤ Defining a method for interpersonal sharing

➤ Developing a community calendar

These steps are not accomplished in any particular order and some decisions may influence the outcome of another area. For example, a mothers' group is emerging and they may decide to meet once a week, during the day, in rotating homes due to childcare.

As the community matures, its identity will crystallize. You may lose some members because it wasn't what they 'bargained for'. Don't be discouraged; remember it is the work of the Holy Spirit. In any small community of faith, there will be members who are committed to the survival of the group. It will be at this time that members ask others to join.

A small community of faith is a gathering of people in a group that meets regularly where members can connect their life and faith. They are not necessarily connected to a parish or a congregation. They pray, may share the scriptures, take their spiritual life seriously, support each other, ritualize common values, and have an external life. Out of their community will come personal conversion, a context for social change, and justice for all peoples.

Mary and Elizabeth model for us an example of what can happen when people gather together. The ability to articulate God's presence in the world happens in such gatherings. Time is of the essence in animating and developing different forms of small communities. Remember that Mary stays with Elizabeth for three months. We can only imagine what they did for each other during that time.

Prayer

My soul proclaims the greatness of the Lord
and my Spirit rejoices in my God!
For God has remembered me, a faithful servant.
From now on people will call me blessed
because of the great things God has done for me.
God's name is holy and blessed.

God has shown mercy from one generation to another.
God stretches out a mighty arm and scatters the proud,
brings down the mighty and powerful,
lifts up the lowly and powerless.
God fills the hungry will great things
and the rich will have nothing.

God has kept the promise made to our ancestors long ago,
to Abraham and Sarah and all their children, coming to their aid.

Appendix

Small Group Agreement

In small Christian community we are invited to follow the path of one-anothering to become our best selves individually and communally.

In that spirit we agree:

➤ To keep confidences. We feel secure in sharing our lives openly and honestly with one another because we know what we say will not leave the group.

➤ To make attendance at all gatherings a priority in our lives because we depend on one another to make our group complete.

➤ To arrive on time prepared to participate and focus on the agenda because we value one another's time.

➤ To listen carefully to one another knowing we each hold an important piece of the community which has a life of its own.

➤ To respect one another and resist making comments or correcting or giving advice unless it is requested.

➤ To welcome the diversity in one another's experiences, beliefs, prayer, and lifestyles.

➤ To appreciate silences, tears, conflict and other challenging situations because we have patience with one another and want to grow in love.

➤ To work with one another, to stand with the marginalized, the poor and the oppressed; to critique the causes for these situations and, by virtue of the gospel, to work for justice and dignity of each and every human being.

SCC Brochures, Flyers, Bulletin Announcements, Newsletters

Written materials help pass on the vision of small Christian communities and explain the particular process of community in your parish. Newsletters and bulletin announcements also provide ongoing presence for SCCs.

Follow the general rules for creating effective marketing materials in print. Use simple language, short sentences and paragraphs, personal stories, and lots of white space. A well-placed quote can help get your point across and provide credibility.

Use any materials in this book, but give proper credit to the originators, the book, and to Good Ground Press. You may also find the following resources useful.

One-Anothering Statements in the New Testament

➤ So we, though many, are one Body in Christ and individually members one of another (Romans 12.5). Clothe yourselves, all of you, with humility toward one another (1 Peter 5.5).

➤ Therefore comfort one another (1 Thessalonians 4.18).

➤ Encourage one another (Hebrews 10.25).

➤ Bear one another's burdens (Galatians 6.2).

➤ Do not speak evil against one another (James 4.11).

➤ May the God of steadfastness and encouragement grant you to live in harmony with one another (Romans 15.5).

➤ Welcome one another as Christ has welcomed you (Romans 15.7).

➤ Therefore encourage one another and build one another up (1 Thessalonians 5.11).

➤ Practice hospitality ungrudgingly to one another (1 Peter 4.9).

Quotable SCC Quotes

"We are not meant to live in isolation. From the beginning God's will was that we be a community of brothers and sisters without divisions; there can be differences that enrich, yes, divisions no. The message of scripture is clear: no barriers. This theme is taken up by Paul who makes a creative theological leap in Galatians 3.28 to declare: There is neither Jew nor Greek, there is neither slave nor free, there is neither male nor female, for all are one in Christ Jesus."

—James O'Halloran, SDB, *Small Christian Communities: Vision and Practicalities*

"The Spirit enters into a community when, through its members' common yearning, the community opens itself and makes itself ready to be Spirit-driven."

— Eberhard Arnold, *Why We Live in Community*

"For most active U.S. Catholics, the Sunday Eucharist is their experience of gathering. It is not uncommon for a Catholic to attend Sunday Mass and not know the people on either side, in front or in back—in which case we do not experience ourselves as part of a community that has chosen to gather in celebration of what God is doing among us together."

— Bernard J. Lee, SM, *The Catholic Experience of Small Christian Communities*

"It's easy to see the Church as the hierarchy, as the priests and sisters who taught us. It's more difficult to learn that we make up the church…that we make up the body of Christ, each of us as different parts of it. The pope is a member of the Church and I'm a member of the Church and we both have our responsibilities in the Church.

— Nora Petersen, *Small Christian Communities; What a Way to Go*

RESOURCES

For ongoing help choosing SCC resources, subscribe to the *Buena Vista Resource Page.*

ORGANIZATIONS

Buena Vista
PO Box 745475 Arvada CO 80006
Phone: 303-477-0180 Fax: 303-477-0179
E-mail: bv@buenavista.org **www.buenavista.org**
    Buena Vista is a national, Catholic, grassroots network of people who have advocated for the formation and support of small Christian Communities since 1987. Buena Vista provides newsletters, *Buena Vista Ink* and *Resource Page* to members six times a year and hosts annual convocations. The website offers peer encouragement, unique resources and local networking opportunities.

Maitland-Newcastle Diocese
Paul O'Bryan, Diocese of Maitland-Newcastle
PO Box 756, Newcastle NSW 2300, Australia
paul.o'bryan@mn.catholic.org.au
    Paul O'Bryan and staff offer various services including publications designed to help understand the SCC vision, call forth animators and accompaniers, begin the journey, and answer questions.

Marianist Lay Network of North America (MLNNA);
Center for Marianist Spirituality and Communities (SMSC)
1341 N. Delaware Avenue #302A
Philadelphia, PA 19125-4300
Phone: 215-634-4116   MLNNA@aol.com or **www.mlnna.com**
    The MLNNA is a network of small communities of faith developed and formed in the Marianist tradition. Members are individuals and small communities. MLNNA is the official North American branch of the worldwide Marianist Family.
    The primary mission of CMSC is the development and formation of SCCs in the Spirit of Mary and the Marianist tradition.

National Alliance of Parishes Restructuring into Communities (NAPRC)
310 Allen Street, Dayton, OH 45410
Phone: 937-256-3600   Fax: 937-256-7138
E-mail: naprcoffice@ameritech.net   **www.naprc.faithweb.com**
We are an alliance of parishes committed to a new vision of being church. This vision is framed in the goal of building an atmosphere in which ordinary people help each other connect their life and faith regularly by doing the things we do differently and forming small Church communities.

National Pastoral Life Center (NPLC)
18 Bleecker Street, New York, NY 10012-2404
Phone: 212-431-7825   Fax: 212-274-9786
E-mail: smallcommunities@nplc.org   **www.nplc.org**
Our approach is to build community, faith reflection, and action through already existing ministries, organizations, and societies, as well as through seasonal and ongoing SCCs.

New Way of Being Church
c/o The Palace, Wells, Somerset, England, BA5 2PD
Telephone: 44-01749 683143
E-mail: randsrymer@aol.com   **www.newway.org.uk**
New Way is a network of people who seek to cooperate with Jesus Christ in the formation of God's new order of justice, love, and peace. We encourage people engaged in transforming the places where they live and work into communities of hope. We provide workshops, publications, a resource library, and website.

North American Forum for Small Christian Communities
c/o Sr. Patricia Froning, OSF, Chairperson, NAFSCC Board
600 Locust Street, Owensboro KY 42301   Phone: 270-683-1545
E-mail: pat.froning@pastoral.org   **www.nafscc.org**
The North American Forum for small Christian communities is a membership organization for Canadian and U.S. diocesan representatives involved in the ministry of small Christian communities.

North American Forum on the Catechumenate
Sr. Sheila O'Dea, 3033 Fourth St NE, Washington, D.C. 20017-1102
E-mail: sodea@naforum.org
Information about recent collaborative parish and diocesan efforts
between the RCIA process and small Christian communities.

Parish Renewal Consulting Services
Betsy Lamb, 5630 Oakland Mills Road, Columbia, MD 21045
Phone: 443-367-0257   E-mail: PRCS@comcast.net
The mission of PRCS is to help parishes, dioceses, small communities, and other faith groups to become People Renewing Church and Society. Bilingual workshops, training materials, and strategic planning are available.

RENEW International
1232 George Street, Plainfield, NJ 07062
Phone: 908-769-5400 Fax: 908-769-5660
E-mail: Deirdre@renewintl.org **www.renewintl.org**
Since 1978, RENEW International, through its RENEW processes, has touched the lives of over 25 million people in dynamic Sunday liturgies, personal meditation, family reflection, and small communities for faith sharing, prayer, and action

MATERIALS ABOUT SMALL CHRISTIAN COMMUNITIES
Phone numbers are provided for distributors not listed above.

Beginning the SCC Journey, Paul O'Bryan (Diocese of Maitland-Newcastle)

Catholic Experience of Small Christian Communities, Bernard Lee (Paulist Press, 800-218-1903)

Changing Communities: Church From the Grassroots, Jeanne Hinton and Peter B. Price (CTBI, **www.chbookshop.co.uk**)

Creating Small Church Communities, Fr. Art Baranowski (National Alliance of Parishes Restructuring Into Communities)

Discerning Leaders for the Small Church Group, Paul O'Bryan (Diocese of Maitland-Newcastle)

Facilitating a Small Group/Animado los Grupos Pequenas, Donna Ciangio, OP (National Pastoral Life Center)

One-Anothering, Volume 2, Rev. Richard C. Meyer, (Innisfree Press, 800-367-5872)

Pastoring the Small Christian Community, Betsy Lamb (Parish Renewal Consulting Services)

Small Christian Communities: A Vision for the 21st Century, Fr. Tom Kleissler, Margo LeBert, Mary McGuinness (RENEW)

Small Christian Communities: Group Dynamics and Facilitation Training, Office of Catholic Faith Formation, Archdiocese of Seattle (800-950-4970)

Small Church Communities: Imagining Future Church, Robert Pelton, CSC (Notre Dame Press, 800-621-2736)

Small Christian Communities: Vision and Practicalities, James O'Halloran, SDB (Columba Press, **www.columba.ie**)

The Big How-To Book for Small Church Communities, Betsy Lamb (Parish Renewal Consulting Services)

Towards An African Narrative Theology, Joseph G. Healey, MM, Donald Sybertz, MM (Orbis Books, 800-258-5838)

What Kind of Small Community Are You? Donna Ciangio, OP (National Pastoral Life Center)

MATERIALS FOR SMALL CHRISTIAN COMMUNITIES

These resource materials generally include everything needed for a small-group session and are very easy for beginning groups and new facilitators to use.

An Experience of World Church in Miniature, Robert K. Moriarty, SM (Diocese of Hartford, 467 Bloomfield Ave., Bloomfield, CT 66002, 860-243-9642; Fax: 860-286-0289; info@sccquest.org)

Brendan Book of Prayer for Small Groups, James O'Halloran, SDB (Columba Press, **www.columba.ie**)

Designing Ritual: Celebrating the Sacred in the Ordinary, Fr. James Telthorst, Richard White, Felicia Wolf, OSF (Buena Vista/Living the Good News, 800-824-1813)

Faith Sharing for Small Church Communities, (National Alliance of Parishes Restructuring Into Communities)

Family Faith Communities: 10 Ready-to-Use-Gatherings, Amy Sluss (Good Ground Press, 800-232-5533, **www.good-ground press.com**)

Getting a Grip On Your Group, Barbara A. Darling (Good Ground Press, 800-232-5533, **www.goodgroundpress.com**)

Impact Series, (RENEW International)

Living Scripture: Connecting to the Great Story, Rick Connor, SM, Nora Petersen, Richard Rohr, OFM (Buena Vista/Living the Good News, 800-824-1813)

Reading the Signs of the Times: A Seven-Week Small-Group Process for Social Change, Nora Petersen, Stephen Hicken, Hector Medina (Resource Publications, 408-287-8748 info@rpinet.com)

Seeking Justice: Participating in the Public Life of Faith, Peter Eichten, Michael A. Cowan, Bernard Lee, SM (Buena Vista/ Living the Good News, 800-824-1813)

Ubi Caritas: Where There is Love and Caring for Others, There is God, Barbara Howard, William V. D'Antonio (Buena Vista/ Living the Good News, 800-824-1813)

LECTIONARY-BASED, FAITH-SHARING MATERIALS

Also complete and easy for new groups and facilitators to use.

Sunday by Sunday, Joan Mitchell, CSJ, editor (Good Ground Press, 800-232-5533; **www.goodgroundpress.com**)

Celebrating the Word, Frank Ruetz, CR (**celebratingtheword.com**)

Exploring the Sunday Readings (Twenty-Third Publications, 800-321-0411)

Prayer Time; Faith Sharing Reflections on the Sunday Gospels— Cycle A, B or C (RENEW International)

Quest, Robert K. Moriarty and other writers (Diocese of Hartford, 860-243-9642; info@sccquest.org)

God's Word Is Alive! Entering the Sunday Readings, Alice E. Camille (Twenty-Third Publications)

VIDEOS FOR AND ABOUT SMALL CHRISTIAN COMMUNITIES

2020 Vision for the Parish (National Alliance of Parishes Restructuring into Communities)

It's a Small Church After All (Ven Con Nosotros) (Buena Vista)

Parish Core Communities Video Series (RENEW International)

Small Christian Communities; What a Way to Go! (Buena Vista)

OTHER RESOURCES

2002 Global Research Project on Small Christian Communities
Bob Pelton, Anne Reissner, Barb Darling, Coordinators
Forty-two SCCs in 14 different countries contributed to this informal study sponsored by Kellogg Institute, University of Notre Dame and Center for Mission Research and Study at Maryknoll. The entire body of research is available on the web at **www.buenavista.org**

Good Ground Press
The publishing arm of the Sisters of St. Joseph of Carondelet in St. Paul, Minnesota, Good Ground Press has an award-winning website that offers prayers of the day and several online retreats, including retreats for Advent and Lent and one on writing one's memoirs. The site links to organizations that work on justice issues. Resources can be viewed and ordered online.

Communities Australia (Newsletter)
www.palms.org.au/CA.htm

Diocese of Hobart, Tasmania
Contact Ms. Eva Dunn about several good resources written especially for SCCs. eva.dunn@cdftas.com

Project Link Up Website
This site promotes the model of adult initiation developed in the
Melbourne, Australia, Catholic Parish of St. Thomas More,
Belgrave, where the catechumenate has been relocated into parish
Small Church Communities. **home.vicnet.net.au/~rciascc**

Regather the Parish
(SCC Newsletter, Diocese of Melbourne, Australia)
Contact Brian and Sandra Mitchell bmitchel@bigpond.net.au

Twist in the Tale: Parables from the Neighborhood Church
(Newsletter) **www.adelaide.catholic.org.au/Services/BEC**

SCCs in African Culture
www.maryknollafrica.org

SCC Twinning
SCC twinning is a mutual giving and sharing between two small
groups from different cultures and countries. It is a great way for
small groups to connect with the larger church and community, help
promote world peace, and establish the Body of Christ. This is a
very grassroots movement with several folks offering to help connect SCCs with one another around the world.
Contact: badarling@juno.com or JGHealey@aol.com

AUTHORS

To contact the authors of this book:

Barbara Darling
3731 Myers Lane
St. James City, FL 33956
239-283-0446
badarling@juno.com

Jack Ventura, SM
The Marianists
Office of Religious Life
4425 West Pine Blvd.
St. Louis, MO 63108-2301
314-533-1207
jventura@sm-usa.org
www.marianist.com